MW00714877

Kindling the Light

For additional copies, contact the author:
WordEtching@gmail.com
Give feedback and join the conversation:
www.WordEtching.com

Cover design: Karla Doell

ISBN: 978-0-9936368-0-6

EmPress Printers and Publishers

Sometimes our light goes out
but is blown again into flame
by an encounter with another human being.
Each of us owes the deepest thanks
to those who have rekindled this inner light.

~ Albert Schweitzer

Foreword

Why do we write poetry? Why do we read?

Enter the world of words and ideas shared by someone who has been penning poems since she was old enough to write. Karla Doell inspires others to pay attention, capture fleeting beauty and embrace wholehearted living. Her purpose is to convince and persuade; her hope is for us to analyze—and challenge—cherished perspectives.

Karla values creative writing. She does not believe the lie that poetry is merely for poets—everything can be poetic. Blithely she breaks away from routine structures and explores free verse while maintaining the coherence and creativity of more traditional poetic forms.

She writes with empathy and compassion; she is contemplative, thoughtful—and thought-provoking. Many of her poems require only a willing reader to appreciate them; others leave room for serious reflection and interpretation.

Without hesitation I encourage you to accept the invitation from a gifted GirlPoet to step into a new world, a new way of seeing.

Elaine M. Phillips
Adjunct Instructor, English and History
Cochrane, Canada
March 2014

Preface

With the creation of this book, I am kindling the light of poetry and photography. The content is aimed at everyone willing to take a moment to think, appreciate, cry or love in a new way. I want each reader to feel one compelling emotion, to experience one new perspective.

All the poems were written after Grade 12 graduation, with one exception. Some of the poems were assigned to me by my English instructor while I was enrolled at a local college. I continued writing after the semester ended, and later my prof and I met weekly at a neighbourhood coffee shop. She provided the hot chocolate; I provided the poems. At the end of 2012 I had a large enough collection for a book, and a one-of-a-kind copy was printed and presented to my parents as a special gift. That first collection remains unique, but the time has come to share my work with a larger audience.

Karla Doell

Acknowledgements

I would like to thank my mentor, Elaine Phillips,
for her cheerful accountability and encouragement;
without her this anthology would never have seen the light.

Thank you to my siblings, David and Jeremy,
for permission to use their photographs in this book,
and to Kiera, for posing in some of the photos.

Thank you to my family
for being supportive
and at times
a muse (d).

Shall I Dedicate This to You?

The first time it was inspiring
to see a book dedicated to the Lord.
Now I've seen so many.
Is it the fruit of an unspoken rule—
simply the proper thing to do?

All of creation is Yours.
My dedication does not change that
the page, the ink, the mind and the soul
that birthed this book belonged to You
before I opened my tiny eyes
and saw the world for the first time.

All of mine is Yours:
all that I craft, whether
written, knitted, painted,
or chiselled in stone...

Will this act appear to be only
a replica of someone else's mould?
Or is it obedience to a Saviour and King
by His child and follower?

The words themselves change nothing. Still—
I dedicate this book in my heart and spirit.

Contents

Starry Sky   **8**
Beautifully Made   9
Sheath(ed)   10
Waiting   11
Cleansing   12
Too Early   13
Knowing and *Knowing*   14
Old Friend, New Friend   15
Legacy   16
All I Have   17
Invitation   18
Many Are Called   20

Kindling   **21**
Newspaper   22
Communication Error   23
Left and Right   24

Cheese Puffs   25
Damsel in Distress /   26
Royal in Revolt   27
Sleep   28
Skipping Time   29
I'm Dreaming of Reality   30

Bark, Twigs, Chaff   31
Red Light   32
Ephemeral   33
Charity   34
Age Identity   35
Clean Dishes   36

Leaves, Moss, Pine Cones   37
Not Just a Flower   38
Your Forty-Five   40
I Am All the Colours   42
It's People   43
How Are You?   44
When No One Is Watching   45

Contents

Stone Circle **46**
What If I Told You 47
Watermelon Seeds 48
Ball in the Yard 50
Door Frame 51
Slate 52
Glade 53

Fire **54**
Not a Poem 55
The Blank Page 56

Logs **57**
The Perfect Season 58
Elaine Phillips 60
Engineer's Birthday 61
Hug 62

Embers/Coal/Ash **63**
For the Rest of Us 64
How Do I Say Goodbye? 65
Shadow 66
The Sound 68
Satan's Roller Coaster 70
Too Weak to Stand 72
Temptation 73
If Only 74

Sparks **75**
Summer Skies 76
Autumn 77
Reprieve 78
Waves of Sand 79
Warm Snowfall 80
Lily Rose 81
Shells of the Ocean 82

Starry Sky

BEAUTIFULLY MADE

W
  E

   A
   R
    E

Burdened by
Every yearning
Anchored to our spirit;
Unwilling to accept our
Thirst for living water or find
Intimacy with Him who provides it;
Fallen creatures we became, but you are
Urged to discover the truth and embrace the
Love and laughter that comes from
Learning how
You were

    M
    A
     D
      E

Sheath(ed)

A metal Bible is quite neat,
Its impact you decide;
For its purpose is incomplete
Without the words inside.

Waiting

Terminal; sit, linger
Fidgeting, tired
Others pace around
The voice calls:
Arise! Arise!

Cleansing

Droplets shimmering in the sun
      fleck across
      my cheek.

Cool and refreshing,
a brook beneath
      my feet.

Flowing down,
not left to right—
      but mind
      to heart.

Spirit to spirit—
from the heavens
      to His
      work of art.

This whisper
      is
      tranquillity.

An awesome flood
      cleanses
      all iniquity.

Profound purity of vision
      reveals in me
      victory.

This declaration skyward
      should be
      contradictory.

But none of it compares
to the truth within it all—
love from the beginning of time
      conquers all.

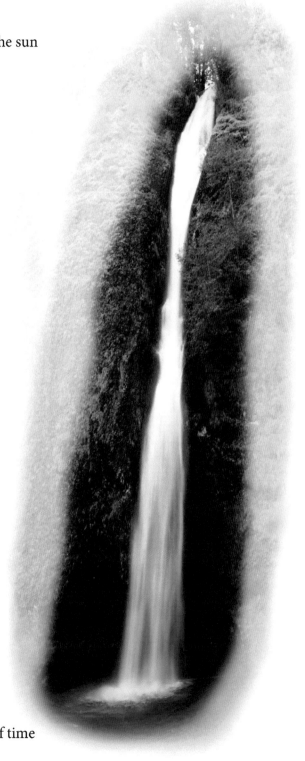

Too Early

God is in the waking moments

In the dawn and
in the darkness

In the still quiet place
where intimate sharing waits to envelop you
in hushed tones like a hug

While you sleep He is there

The one who spoke the universe into existence
knit you together in your mother's womb
and conquered death for you

He wants to know you
and you, Him

He waits in the day
but does not sleep
while the Earth rotates
its back to the sun

Is He calling on you
during closed eyes
to wake for Him?

Knowing and *Knowing*

I know He loves me.
It's a fact.
I have read and heard it,
but never react.

Talked to someone once,
who knew it in her heart.
A power swelling and pouring out—
made it impossible to fall apart.
A wrapping pure in comfort,
safety and caring.
A time undefiled,
filled with intimate sharing.

I know of Him.
But if I knocked on Stranger's gate,
I'd be denied in attempting
to move into His estate.
There are no rights for me to claim,
for I know nothing more
than a book and His name.

"Will you grasp my hand?
Hold me close?"
What I know is true—
The last breath escapes my lips:
"Now I want to *know* You."

Old Friend, New Friend

Alpha, Creator, chronicled at the dawn,
Nestled with blankies that muffle my yawn,
He is exalted as bedtime stories read till dreaming,
The guardian nightlight amplifies my heartfelt gleaming.

I read the lines, I look to the core
So many times, but what's that there?
Contemplate, meditate, I sit and stare,
Something new I did not notice before.

A mountain, an ocean, the stars with great majesty,
Today I enquire, how long have they been?
Today I marvel at the glories within,
Why design such awesome beauty for me?

Old friend, new friend

There in the beginning
There in my beginning
An old friend Who every day is new

Legacy

They speak;
I preach the love of Jesus,
and am thrown in jail.

They write classics;
I write for Jesus,
and am left on the shelf.

They direct blockbusters;
I film a piece for Jesus—
Will anyone even hear of it?

They draw a line in the sand;
I draw battle lines against the enemy,
and find myself standing alone.

They publish history;
I clarify that Jesus works in the present,
and am persecuted.

They sleep in their private house;
I lay my head where there are open homes,
and find there are fewer every year.

They live;
I tell them how Jesus lived,
and am crucified.

Movies fade
Books are lost
Speeches forgotten

But what I do for You
lasts an eternity.

All I Have

I have no skip in my step or a hug-loaded gun,
No happiness in here—and you might poke fun.

All I have is a joy, nestled warmly in my heart,
Birthed by hope and by truth, which is the greatest part.

I have not riches, glory, mansions, land or fame,
But in the Book of Life, He has written my name.

I will never be on top, the first of any line,
Because I am one of the branches of His vine.

I will never be well known or have the world's adoration.
All I have is Eternity, His saving-grace-gift of salvation.

I have no assistants or coaches to tell me of my worth,
Just the endless verses of why my King came to Earth.

His awesome love comes to supersede;
This is all I have—and this is all I need.

In all the nations: cities, rocks, hills and sea,
All I have is Jesus; He is sufficient for me.

Invitation

The crunching of crystals
underfoot in the night,
bells to hang
and candles to light.

Ten thousand cards to copy out
before the season even starts;
so this is where we mass produce
the muses of our hearts.

Each store has gifts
of every sort of twinkle,
wrapped for show
and for curious hands to crinkle.

Not enough time with family gifts
to make and find;
there are also neighbours and friends
to keep in mind.

Insert
Your
Christmas
Photo
Here

One party (or two)
to attend every week,
baking when time allows
with tasty samples to eat.

Beckoning trees and festivities
on every street, in every store,
but what about that Child:
the one this is all for?

It is a remembrance
of His birth;
why is that
so unclear?

A choir of angels
did herald the Gift of love;
on that blessed night
the Lamb of God did appear.

I think it's time
to invite Jesus
for Christmas
this year.

Insert
Your
Christmas
Photo
Here

Many Are Called

Scott lives in a town with a gas station and church

He went to school, found a job and paid taxes on time
He worked his way up to head agriculture research
And was later promoted to travel on company dime

With skills and life experience well in hand
God came and gave him a personal task
Scott fell to his knees and obeyed the command
But found himself troubled and needing to ask,

"Why me? Why not the greats?
The presidents and CEOs and
Those who possess large estates?"

And God replied, "Because
you are the only one
who answered."

Kindling

Kindling

Newspaper

(0mmμn1(4710n— 3rr0r

When I say—
I'm kindling the light,
Know that I'm not using an e-book to light my way.

When I say—
You should eat blackberries,
Realize that picking microprocessors from your teeth is not okay.

When I say—
The 10 Commandments were written on tablets at Mount Sinai,
Don't picture a computer being smashed to turn people back to Adonai.

When I say—
Check the clouds to know the coming weather,
Then every calendar is in your palm, altogether.

When I say—
Tweet me a song today that is filled with kind words,
What I receive is not something in the language of birds.

At what point did your brain make the switch?
Remember that when I say—When I say—When I say—
My repetition is not a computer glitch.

Left   and   Right

It is war:
There are two sides,
One is Tefl, one is Tirgh;
They are brothers.

Tefl is structure, logic, rules,
Mathematics, physics.
Tefl builds a box and lives inside the box,
He boils water in the box,
And builds aeroplanes in the box.

> Tirgh is creativity, imagination,
> He dreams dreams, tells stories, and paints pictures.
> Tirgh brings discs of iridescent light into Tefl's box
> And shatters it into infinite pieces.
> He dances into the sky,
> And dives to the depths of the earth.

> Tirgh figured out the meaning of the brothers' names,
> Tefl enquired of their parents to receive the answer.
> Tefl leashes Tirgh by thinking he is unrealistic—
> And stops believing he exists.
> Then Tirgh cannot leave, and so continues to pester Tefl.

They are two halves of the same whole:
In this place one cannot live without the other,
> Destined to be locked in combat for eternity,
> Or at the very least, until the place ceases to exist.

Kindling

Cheese Puffs

Damsel in Distress

I am a board girl,
25 years since Berth.
I billed castles quite often;
they withstand anything.
Don't listen to Dad if he speaks of that one time where it didn't
because we can debate all day weather
the sky blue wright threw the seller with a creek—
or NOT
and I don't have the time for such small talk.

Today a night entered the castle and sang to me;
I told him,
If the plane doesn't sweep you off your feet,
why lye that I do?

The last guy said to me,
"Too much wait."
I said, "Shoot"
and he went down with the waist.

You, sir, have not one my hart.
If you continue to strike a cord with me, deer,
the made will be scent for, to toe you to see,
oar perhaps throw you in the dungeon.
Inside I warn you knot to hug bare
because he eight at nine—
yesterday.

Chews to leave
four you are not aloud
to take my hand in marriage.

There is a storm in the straight now.
Wood be a pity
to see you brake your neck on a bolder.

Royal in Revolt

I am a bored girl,
25 years since birth.
I build castles quite often;
they withstand anything.
Don't listen to Dad if he speaks of that one time where it didn't
because we can debate all day whether
the sky blew right through the cellar with a creak—
or NOT
and I don't have the time for such small talk.

Today a knight entered the castle and sang to me;
I told him,
If the plain doesn't sweep you off your feet,
why lie that I do?

The last guy said to me,
"Too much weight."
I said, "Chute"
and he went down with the waste.

You, sir, have not won my heart.
If you continue to strike a chord with me, dear,
the maid will be sent for, to tow you to sea,
or perhaps throw you in the dungeon.
Inside I warn you not to hug Bear
because he ate at nine—
yesterday.

Choose to leave
for you are not allowed
to take my hand in marriage.

There is a storm in the strait now.
Would be a pity
to see you break your neck on a boulder.

Sleep

Sleep
Lovely, necessary
Dreaming, breathing, floating
The most beautiful experience
Unattainable

Skipping Time

Skip... Skip... Skip...

Can water skip on water?
But someone asked
why does it have to be a stone?
Snow curled up tight
thrown precisely just right
Be careful not to accept
the ripples past kept
Yes, it can—

Skip... Skip... Skip...

I'm Dreaming of Reality

Dear John Smith:

I'm dreaming of reality
Where apples fall from apple trees

Gravity never decides to takes a vacation
and mice are not bribed in saving the nation

Where the stars always visit the lonely sky
and a flame without a party is always too shy

Where monsters of claw and teeth,
rugged knots of fur and bone-shattering strength
stay locked in nightmares
peaking through closet slits

Where the world does not need to be saved every other day
Why can't it stay saved, just once, in the Milky Way?

Where aliens don't fall from the sky and pick up a rhyme
and people don't alternate-dimension-dabble in their free time

Where I don't discover my wife is a shape shifter
and time travel doesn't tear holes in the fabric of space

Where dragons don't need slaying
or talk in your mind
and humans save animal lives
not the other way round

Where there is only one of me
oh, what a relief that would be
and only my old control freak decorator
cares what colour the roses are

Sincerely,
The Fictional Traveller

Kindling

Bark, Twigs, Chaff

Red Light

The Smart Car
Minivan
Ford Escape
BMW Hatchback
and Corvette Convertible
all drive on the same road

Ford follows half a car behind Smart Car
but doesn't pass when it moves to the new lane

Minivan doesn't accelerate to 100 fast enough
and is passed by the Corvette weaving ahead

BMW cuts into the fast lane without signalling
forcing the drivers behind to brake

Someone has their music blaring
(it's not hard to guess who)

Count how many drivers
glance down to secretly text

Red Light

Corvette doesn't slow till the last second
Minivan comes in 20 seconds late
but they all have to stop
and idle side by side

Side by side

Ephemeral

She falls

He observes life.
"This thing that has fallen from above
whispers in sleep of something called stars,
as if there could be more than one.
Curious how its chest moves
inhaling and exhaling the air."

She awakes

He points to her chest.
"What is it you do, there?"

She speaks

> To breathe,
> I breathe.
> She breathes,
> I am breathing.
> Others have breathed
> before me—or is it
> that they will breathe?

She steps close

> My breath graces your cheek.
> The tide of air shatters as glass.
> I choke—
> It's beautiful here.

She sleeps

He looks to the heavens.
"What was that vapour?"

Charity

Care
Debate
Fair
Estimate

Demonstrate
Observation
Escalate
Cooperation

Toleration
Rain
Donation
Sustain

Appear
Sincere

Age Identity

Who am I?

When I turn Jamie
I am no longer Madison,
but I do not feel like I'm Jamie.
It is strange when someone asks my age.
I think for an awkward moment and answer, "Emily."
A year later Emily almost feels like my real age,
but now I am Kate.
Kate is unfamiliar, an alien sound on my lips,
a distant idea of a stranger.
Yet, it is the truth.

Then I am an adult,
from one day to the next everything changes,
and nothing.
I'm still the same person.
I don't feel different.
I'm not different.
Courtney to Lorraine to Abigail...
no age is mine.
Last year is too distant,
this year is too fresh.

It's my birthday.
"How old are you?" they ask.
You tell me.

Clean Dishes

The dishes are clean!
The dishes are clean!

No, the secret is not
that I'm high on caffeine.
What I'm trying to say
is that the family is—
looking a little lean.

There's nothing in the fridge
gone to waste or going green.
There's no steak, noodles or barley;
not one morsel, grain or bean.

Now I wish there were dishes
for me to clean.

Dirty dishes
are the gift unseen.

Clean floor.
Clean floor.
There are no children
anymore.

Kindling

Leaves, Moss, Pine Cones

Not Just a Flower

Recall for me a moment—

A daughter's fifth Christmas:
Marked by the pink ribbon,
hugging tight the halcyon lights,
suspended on the auburn mantel.

Marriage to the one and only:
Signified by bands of gold,
Circles of perpetual unity,
Prevalent image of love.

Snowed in with the family:
Evidence in an explosion of shimmering doves,
The only image on the single photo attempted,
From "Let go!" to getting to know, in choked closeness.

A close one's depart:
Embodied in the melody of her favourite song,
its recording dances through the empty halls,
invoking profound joy and sorrow.

The battle for an idea:
Indicated by words etched on paper,
Standing firm for what they believed,
To stretch lasting into the grey future.

A speech once given:
Now indicated in quotes,
Spread down through the generations,
In songs, books, education and Internet.

Freedom fought for and claimed:
Remembered by the red poppy,
which makes its home on the graves
of those who sacrificed everything,
amplifying the blood spilt to acquire it.

What is a symbol good for
If the memory is not important,
If a symbol invokes no response,
If it transforms us less than dust on Jupiter?

Then is it anything more than a sham?
A fragment of coloured cloth,
Aurum forged to accessorize a finger,
A blurry photo that never turned out,
A song repeated to redundancy,
An old document to be shelved away,
Words spoken to preoccupied ears of indifference,
A red velvet cut-out pinned to your suit,
the result of conformity, obedience or habit.

It is not the symbol,
But what the symbol represents.
So if we remember
Not just facts, pictures or stories
Out of conformity, obedience or habit,
But instead the deep transforming "Why?"

If on your heart you pin
Not just a flower,
But penetrate your heart
With their selfless sacrifice—

It makes all the difference.

Your Forty-five

Go ahead, gift to me your great knowledge
from all the things you've seen and done.
Eighteen! and already your bias is won.
Oh, and the classes and lectures you've attended!
Does your new prejudice make you apt or clever?
Will you make those youthful ideals last forever?

I am your forty-five

I know you,
and in twenty-seven years
you will be me.
But right now I'm you,
you—
and much, much more.

I am your forty-five

I once held fast that doctrine
that made me so self-right
as to see in only black and white.
I missed out on sharing with some of God's children
and in the corners of the world shine His light.
That is the part I would rewrite.

I am your forty-five

I've already faced the impossible choices
that on your own path are presently unseen.
It is troubling to know that you are a teen,
still to carry the consequences of mistakes
which you have yet to face,
like the testing of your faith.

Who is your forty-five?
What would they do or tell you?

Would they give you the choices
to prevent the disaster
and give you a hug
and small finger wave—
or let it all happen,
and leave the storm
that matured you
for you alone to brave?

I Am All the Colours

I am all the colours:

Am I black?
Am I white?

Red is strength:
anger, sorrow,
sacrifice, loss,
hope and love.

Orange is spontaneous:
lightning energy, innovation,
a million stars in the sky,
and you must connect the dots.

Yellow is being and choosing:
loyalty, respect, courage,
faith, ignorance, humility,
disobedience, selflessness and greed.

Green is structured:
Rules that both bind and protect,
using facts and data,
building balance and foundation.

Blue, the guide:
Twisted duo of knowledge and experience,
words of wisdom and encouragement.
Step by step, the right path.

Violet is image turned mirage:
Tradition, experiences, past companionship.
The important ones are treasured
so that they cannot fade away.

The spectrum of the rainbow merges into white;
the six paints of the pallet mix into black.

I am all the colours:
Am I white?
Am I black?

It's People

You can play with blocks,
paint Pandora's box,
Blog—
or just monologue.
Climb the best peak,
gaze at views every week.
Pound the perfect tune
to tap feet all afternoon.
Win awards for acrobatic stunt,
or even
discover life's great treasure hunt.
All in all take ten
with every free pen.

It's all stuff.
It makes no difference.

It's People.

When the sun shines through
I'll frolic with you.
In the morning light,
I'll paint strokes of
love's first kiss
till deepest night.
Whispers of secrets
in cosy corners,
of experiences shared,
of days yet to share.
Panoramas only witnessed
through uncompromising unity.
Uncover the mysteries,
by way of a medal chewed
with six-month-old teeth.
Laugh at your jokes till
I fall into ocean blue.
The melody that lulls,
it fills the halls,
or makes you prance
in crowds of fiery expanse,
the joy of life—
of living—
of—
A Life Worth Living.

It's People.

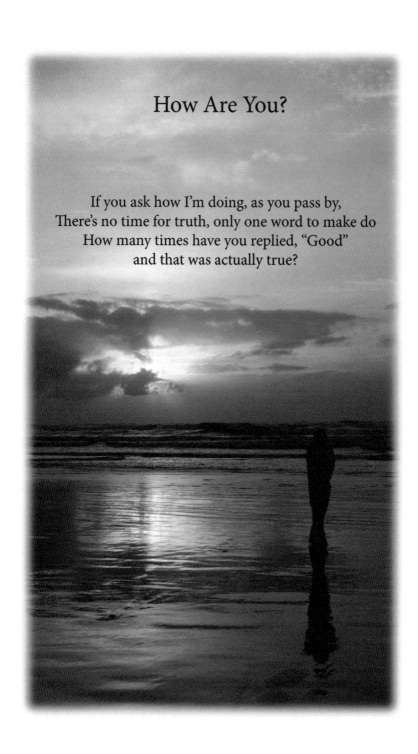

How Are You?

If you ask how I'm doing, as you pass by,
There's no time for truth, only one word to make do
How many times have you replied, "Good"
and that was actually true?

When No One Is Watching

When no one is watching,
The popular girl, the life of the party who seems to have it made,
Stands wishing she could have the courage to dispel her masquerade.

When no one is watching,
The jock, receiving scholarships, who appears to be carefree,
Goes home to be the family's scapegoat appointee.

When no one is watching,
The counsellor and greeter, filling others with comfort and healing,
Needs for once one person to come and ask just how she is feeling.

When no one is watching,
The nerd who eats lunch alone, rejected, and unnoticed when he drops out,
Stays home to care for his sick mother; a husband and father they are without.

When no one is watching,
The reclusive child who shrinks back, will not join in games, and is no fun,
Lives with her uncle, abused and cursed as useless, with nowhere to run.

When no one is watching,
The guy provoking laughter, the quipster, comedian, the famous class clown,
Is a derelict son, spending nights in his truck, his only place to lie down.

When no one is watching,
The boss who pushes employees too hard, is cold and just a plain slave driver,
Mourns the loss of his family in a car crash, he the sole survivor.

Only in muffled shadows can you hear the meadowlark cry out like the crow;
Be for them the fire-lit cabin in the wind-swept tundra;
The gemstone concealed in the thorny crown.

Watch, when no one is else is watching.
Love, when they feel unloved.
See, when everyone else is blind.

Stone Circle

What If I Told You

What if I told you
What you mean to me

I'll wait a while
Till I get it right

Soon, too soon, I'm forced to speak
Weep your eulogy

Here and now they're nice words,
Hear them while you're still alive
It can make all the difference
In ways I never knew

So what if I told you
What you meant to me

If I told you every year
Even though you're only three

Watermelon Seeds

Plop, skitter, onto the plate,
one, two, three,
three watermelon seeds.

Little girl carries them
out into the sun;
little girl plants them
one by one.

Grip the dirt to
dig each nest;
settle them carefully,
let them rest.

Plop, plop, plop,
push the dirt back;
tuck them in,
make it flat.

Pour the hose,
a gallon seems right to drink;
little girls
need not rethink.

Leave and return,
to find nothing again and again;
even after one looong day,
could someone please explain?

Attention slips from memory,
the task is now neglected.
She returns weeks later
to find the unexpected.

Little girl squeals,
"Wow, how enchanting,
watermelon seeds grow into flowers:
ones like Mom loves planting!"

Little girl, little girl,
what a perfect gem.

Be careful not to tell,
you'll spoil it for them.

Ball in the Yard

Something lost
Something found

Something simple
Something round

Bounce it hard
On the ground

Listen to that
Sweet sweet sound

The fence is high
It shoots higher

Use your arms
Climb the wire

Find it quickly
Or we'll be done

Bring it back
Bring the fun

Something lost
Something found

Something simple
Something round

Door Frame

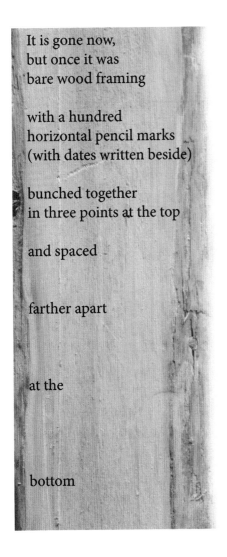

It is gone now,
but once it was
bare wood framing

with a hundred
horizontal pencil marks
(with dates written beside)

bunched together
in three points at the top

and spaced

farther apart

at the

bottom

Now
the
doorway
is
finished,
painted
a perfect
untouched
white,
but not
for long;
the next
generation
is coming

Slate

World, my world
I am,
But who are we?
Define us, ponder us, baffle us

Adulthood distorts perceptions by our
Norms
Character
Viewpoint
Prejudice
Society

Child, my child
You are born the blank slate
onto which the world pours

Time
Image
Emotion
Belief
Value
make an authentic, raw impression
like a leaf trapped in stone

World, my world
The children see
The blank slates reveal

Glade

A girl tip-toes amongst the glimmer of strewn petals
In a glade of thin, pale-blue fog
Five steps to the right
is dark
Her dress spirals as she turns
The petals drift gently, collecting and dispersing
Five steps to the left
is dark
One petal squishes between her bare toes
She stoops down to study it
Five steps backward
is dark
The fog moves off, taking the wind with it
The petals drag themselves, tumbling in attempt to pursue
She lunges forward to save them
But they slip through her fingers
One step forward
is dark

Fire

Not a Poem

At first I was hesitant to write again,
Perhaps out of fear
Of not being as good as before.

But for the second time,
I walk across the field
Which appears to be dead.

It is only playing possum,
In instinctual protection
Against winter's impending reign.

With the wind blinding me,
Whipping the hair into my face,
Again I find my inspiration.

Perhaps this be in part the definition of poetry:
Saying in a hundred words
What could be said in ten.

But not till the hundredth
Do you find the beauty and meaning
In a dead field of grass.

The Blank Page

On the blank page patter lines, curves, dots and circles.
The utensil: raise then return, push and glide,
Together they form patterns and collections.
Add some pauses—because the void
Can, in itself be something.
Mark and rest, thick and slight—
Scarce a trace of hesitation.

The blank page begins to communicate

Longer, longer, racing forward,
Stop. Continue—Stop.
Section by section,
Something symbolic descends onto the page,
Tracing the architecture of a dream.
It aspires in the light
And contemplates in the dark.

The blank page receives meaning

It breathes softly,
Its heart beats in a hushed dance,
It stirs the senses from a deep slumber,
It etches in the mind,
It tickles the heart,
A prism unfurled beyond the visual spectrum,
A melody ablaze in the bones.

The blank page transforms emotion

One stands in awe at the stark contrast:
Framed in a rectangle,
Bound by a writer,
It whispers to the soul.

Logs

The Perfect Season

My favourite season is not spring,
summer,
autumn,
or winter.

To everything there is a season,
a time for every purpose under heaven:
a time to be born, and a time to die...

...a time to
weep, and a
time to laugh;
a time to
mourn, and a
time to dance.

...a time to keep silent, and a time to speak.

Ecclesiastes 3

But it can be experienced in a moment: the moment
when you can stand in the crisp, fresh mountain air
and fill your lungs with the intoxicating scent
of an approaching rain. A moment—
that I wish could last a lifetime.
I find myself forgetting the need
to exhale, before inhaling another breath of
                                        prolonged elation.

Cute, furry creatures are concealed in the underbrush
and with patience they can be skilfully coaxed out.
Beyond the thicket, snow-capped mountains glow
with brilliant, pure morning light; the wind tinkles softly
in an echoing whisper that cannot quite
                                        be grasped.

But a season is more than a physical description.
Seasons are enjoyed and remembered
by social interaction: with family and friends;
even with rivals. In your perfect place,
whether Mexico or the Caribbean
if you are alone,   there is an absence,
                                        an emptiness within.

And so,
in my perfect season I must add my family,
all sitting within the white ancient gazebo
in this mystic forgotten garden, scattered amongst
the shattered stoic pillars. We talk, eat and play games
in the stillness of the dawn. A silence
                                        of loving murmurs.

Elaine Phillips

Engaging in unconventional methods

Laughing to her own beat

A great mentor to me

In gifts once unseen

Never a dull moment with

Endless opportunities to grow

Perhaps dreams filled with

Hippos (and unicorns)

Inconceivable I know, but word-

Lover through and through

Lingering in the brisk autumn dusk

Iambic crystal halos drifting in

Pure waters that mirror

Sky of lapis lazuli

Engineer's Birthday

My dad, the engineer,
You built them all over the years—
Hospitals, depots and Toys 'R' Us-es
Was each completion met with tears,
Relief or resounding cheers?

Across the horizon: highway and railway;
Vertical: a highrise office, too.
Each project you can be proud of,
Each one tried and true.
The greatest one? If only you knew.

It is possible for those buildings to
have their time and disappear.
But the greatest testament to you of all
Are the hearts and lives sitting right here.
Of structure and stability, physics of adversity;
You are ahead on building things that last.
It doesn't matter what you are—
To us you are World Class.

Hug

The grip of woven arms transcend
to mend a circle without end

Between shared tears
is a twinkle in the eyes
where love never fades
and never dies

Embers/Coal/Ash

For the Rest of Us

What is dust on a beach?
Can you distinguish one iota from the grain?

Footsteps
Human imprints
Water leaking in
forming puddles
One divot
for each step
or seven—
is an outcome of pace

Not the end—
one more bridge
one more bend
in the road
More like a path
but uncharted
with flickers to pursue
avoid or defend

Is there a message—

For the rest of us?

How Do I Say Goodbye?

In answer:
The same way you did when
I went to work
or took a trip.

I'm moving
from one room of the house
to the other,
this time with no possessions
slung along.

I'm visiting Father.
I love you,
See you soon.

Shadow

Well?
Say hello.
It is you there.
Don't be rude—you'll make it angry.

How hard is it for you to understand?
The light doesn't hit the ground between you and the sun,
and thus casts a cookie-cutter shape of your soul.

Now you actually get to see it.
You cannot hide from it
or lie about its shape and nature.

Quick! Feed it something
before it goes and talks to your friends.
There's not enough stuff here?
Or you don't think it's good enough?
Well, your neighbour's is much better,
Let's go get his for it.

Now I'm sure you know that it
sleeps beside you in your bed,
accompanies you to the store,
slums with you on the couch,
and catches a ride with you on any outing.

You never noticed it before?
That's strange.
It says you're best friends,
BFFs.

It helped you hide the evidence from Mom and Dad
of the cookies you ate before supper,
helped you download those—
um—
files onto your computer,
helped steer you away from that pedestrian
the night you were a little bit tipsy,
and made sure you did not go back
to the hotel

alone.

Oh, and it has another great story
about when
you—

Why are you panicking?
Don't say those things.
Calm down.

Wait.
Come back.
What are you doing?
You wouldn't do that.
You wouldn't block out the sun and
plunge the whole world into darknes
        just so that no one can see

The Sound

I sit, or lie, or whatever I do,
listening to that which
quivers the wakefulness
of an obscure fragment
of my mind.

I am tired, yearning
to curl up and feel the sweet release of sleep—
But I cannot.

It is impossible to sleep.
I am completely awake,
yet fatigue suffocates me.

The Sound—
physically I could go and end it,
but physiologically I am
completely
incapacitated.

There are people enjoying it,
The Sound.
My innermost being is consumed
to consider the others
and not to make any spectacle
or speak any unkind words
or any speck that could be interpreted in some way
that would cause another human
to feel less—
whole.

I cannot come to a restful state,
nor can I stay awake to accomplish anything of purpose,
for sleep pounds mercilessly at my door while sedating my mind,
and I am totally helpless to end it.
Even though I am physically capable of
stopping the suffering,
I do not—
and I do not fully understand why.

Each of these pressures have to go one way or another:
They pull at me, torment me,
stretch me to insanity
because moment after moment
I am still in the same moment—unable to escape.
Fragmented.
Forever forbidden to fall asleep, a world away from rest
but unable to find the energy to move, think or accomplish anything,
I curse my—
my own psyche that prevents me from stopping it.

Feeble, I cry.
I plug my ears, twist and turn.
Forsaken, I set myself ablaze in my own bed on freezing winter's nights.
I try to think and find something to do, to shut out
the Sound,
but only another Sound can do that,
and I am so very tired.

Anything,
anything to keep me sane for one moment longer
hoping that in the next moment
it will be over.

But every moment
is another moment more
than I can bear.

Satan's Roller Coaster

With glazed eyes you glimpse the Angel of Light.
He beckons with fingers that writhe and jerk;
You obey and settle in the first car of the train,
Intoxicated by his euphoric lull and artful smirk.

Restraints descend like cages and lock secure:
His voice makes you want it, like a siren's song,
But a gruesome sense begins to rot in your gut
As you grasp to determine what is foul and wrong.

Clickety clack, your casual creep commencing
Upon degrading and rusted but well-used wheels:
Achievement, desire, power, money and worth;
You believed they were rock-foundational ideals.

Racing through the jungles you are entangled,
Vice of desire, a buried pleasure, a crystal dust,
Black wisp of demise, burnt paper and cut plastic,
Drink of poison, deed of perpetual broken trust.

Plunging down into the depths of desolation,
Cold, dark and alone, absolute happy arrest.
Imprisoned and unable to save even yourself,
Useless, incompetent, weakness unrepressed.

One beat. Two beat. Three beat.
The heart stills in flinchless terror;
You want it and cannot stop it,
Deciding only by trial and error.

Through the long tunnel that is padded tight,
You fear no one is listening, no one even cares;
No one calls out your name, or hears you cry;
Everyone is caught up in more crucial affairs.

Into the looping fires of jealousy and hate,
Consuming your soul with coal gifts of spite,
Refusing to forgive a brother, not giving in,
Wanting to force on him your own venom bite.

From afar He comes as thunder, riding on eagle wings;
His very presence forces the coaster to s-l-o-w;
He yanks it to a stop, His gaze filled with grief;
He holds out His hand, His cloak made of snow.

However, you know what taking the hand means:
Submission, servanthood, no more halfway.
Giving forth everything, the money, the riot;
So close, yet so far, will you again turn away?

A boy stands watching, hand on the lever,
Lips of candy, tongue of a Labrador Retriever,
With a smile on his face and a shiny gold pen,
He asks quite nicely, "Would you like to ride again?"

Too Weak to Stand

Dreary skies bleed a toxic film onto every defiled surface
And mask the rickety breeding grounds of disease

Deep abyss
Filth in every pore
Grime clogging every vein
Desperation drips into blossoming plume
Air suffocating, breathing earth
Inhaling death, giving birth

The chasm eats
Toil and sweat
Collapse and weep
Too blind to see

Some bones remain
All childhood buried
Where they lay

Sacrifice the ration crumbs
To keep a child alive
One more day

Click, twick, whizz, zimmer, clack
Exhaustion digs its stakes in deep
Boulders lullaby the eyelids close
Blink. Fall. Down.
Crunch of bone, scream and groan
Authentic crimson fabric sown
For the wealthy. Who else can afford?

Some are silent
All forgotten
They barely blink
Lacking energy to think

There are worse things than war
When no one takes a stand

Temptation

Careful...
The shadows creep
On little kitty feet
Stroke the alluring phantom purr
and die

If Only

Lives are not so well built
as stone upon stone
in the framework of achievement.

Reaching forward for no place,
it's nothingness that kills you,
knocks you down, chokes you
till you wake up again.

Clutch it tight,
kidnap the soul,
hold it ransom,
amass from slick hustle.

On the pinnacle of civilization,
the precipice of sanity,
drink, laugh,
inhale grandeur.

Desire. One last breath.
Always straining for one more
till the spasms mark the
dim of fate's last smile.

Still they ask,
"If only."

Sparks

Summer Skies

They know no fear of death
neither do they live, except in our hearts
as we dream

With unbridled grace the sting ray swoops
through gossamer emblems
Each symbol tears, only to disperse
into the contrail of a rocket ship's blast
into infinity

The great dragon looms
glaring down the ravine below
tempered by clouds that roll amid thunder
swept away to dissolve amongst the forgotten

The underbellies of a magnificent phoenix and nutty-eyed squirrel
command the land of the sky
Burning wings arc and collapse
to claw a churning current of frigid air

Shrapnel of the epic battle
forms a new world
of crumbling isles
detaching remnant stones

The decaying cirrus sword ebbs
until only wisps remain
above the fragmenting creatures
myths of old, and future inspirations

A life span
between seconds or minutes
They live, spark
billow, shatter
metamorphose
and
fade
away...

Autumn

A mosaic of gold, orange, russet and auburn
coalesce at the water's edge

The last of the leaves linger on branches
waving goodbye to their mirror image

"Till next year"

Frost preserves every surface as nature's cloak
crisp and sparkling

The water is cool to the touch
on the tipping point of a decision between liquid and ice

"Winter is coming, winter is coming"

Reprieve

The winter bites
at first nipping on the fringe
but after solid weeks it seeps in
Blankets and simple tricks
cannot halt the chattering of teeth
A hunched gait begins your walk
from the weight on your shoulders

Bud in the Thorns

Then it comes
An orchestra heralds its coming
The clouds build an arch declaring its arrival

Light in the Void

It sweeps across the land
melting the snow
lifting spirits
hovering scarcely above freezing
It feels so warm

Butterfly in the Burnt Woods

Your back straightens, the burden lifts
It's the strength to push through
until the next one

A Fleck of Gold Discovered between Black and White

You have not felt warmth
until you have felt a Chinook
Summer is constant
beating down
but this is something else entirely

A Droplet in the Desert
Is Far More Valuable than One Falling on Ocean Shores

Waves of Sand

The waves were a blanket of silk
as they washed up onto me.
I'll sleep all night on my bed of sand
and in the morning I'll wake with glee.

Warm Snowfall

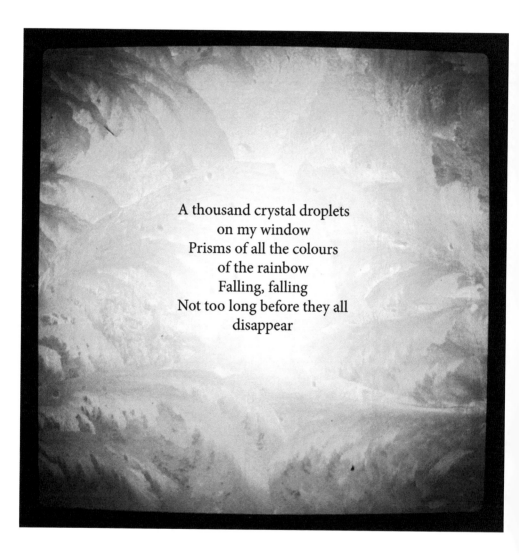

A thousand crystal droplets
on my window
Prisms of all the colours
of the rainbow
Falling, falling
Not too long before they all
disappear

Lily Rose

Softly singing

atop dark waters
to descend and rise on periodic waves
Rocking placid as a baby's cradle
petals of mingling amaranth and amethyst
kiss the water's surface
akin to the bow of a violin
as it graces each string

The sky parts its lips
and a breath of cool mist
eclipses the centre bud
in snow

Shells of the Ocean

I
study
my
handful
of
sand
to
discover
that
children
play
upon
angelic
graveyards

PHOTO CREDITS—AND A ONE-LINE READING GUIDE

Cover design by Karla Doell with three photos credited to David Doell.

Starry Sky – Photo credit: Jeremy Doell
You are *Beautifully Made* is an acrostic poem.
Have you *Sheath(ed)* the sword of the Spirit?
Is *Waiting* on God like a lineup at the airport?
A *Cleansing* can be a moment or a lifetime, salvation or rejuvenation.
   Photo credit: Karla Doell
It's *Too Early* to get up! Did you miss something important?
   Photo credit: David Doell
There's a difference between Knowing and *Knowing*. We all 'know' the
president, but that doesn't get us into the White House.
Daily my God is equally *Old Friend, New Friend*.
   Photo credit: Jeremy Doell
What I do for Christ is my *Legacy*.
All I Have is Jesus. He exceeds all I could possibly need.
Invitation is a Christmas rhyme about the real reason we celebrate.
   Photo credit: _____(insert credit for your personal photo).
Many Are Called by God. Few are listening.

Kindling – Photo credit: Karla Doell
Newspaper – Photo credit: David Doell
The title of *Communication Error* is written in leet [l33t], humorously using
homonyms (same spelling, different meaning) of names for current
technology.
Left and Right deals with the traditional sense of the left(Logic) and
right(Creativity) sides of the brain in conflict during the creative process.
Cheese Puffs – Photo credit: David Doell
The poems *Damsel in Distress / Royal in Revolt* humorously use
homophonic heterographs (words that sound the same but differ in
spelling and meaning). In these two poems, spelling makes all the
difference. Does the damsel need to be saved—or does the knight?
   Photo credit: Karla Doell
If you have ever struggled to *Sleep*, you will understand this brief poem.
Skipping Time, because some people question.
I'm Dreaming of Reality (because it does not receive the credit it deserves).
In reality, fiction is not all superpowers and adventure.

Bark, Twigs, Chaff – Photo credit: Karla Doell

The *Red Light* makes us all equal.

Flowers are *Ephemeral*—and so is life.

       Photo credit: Karla Doell

Charity is a rhyming word sonnet.

I can't keep track of my *Age Identity*.

Be thankful for *Clean Dishes*!

Leaves, Moss, Pine Cones – Photo credit: Karla Doell

The poppy is *Not Just a Flower*. The entities that linger in the aftermath are just symbols. It is not the (symbolic) wedding ring that keeps you faithful. Your = one belonging to you. *Your Forty-Five* is the forty-five-year-old (or current version of) you. It's looking back on yourself or looking forward to the person who will look back on yourself.

       Photo credit: Jeremy Doell

I Am All the Colours is a palette that paints the human being. Does the sum of our parts make us good or evil?

       Photo credit: Jeremy Doell

It's People who make life worth living.

       Photo credit: Jeremy Doell

How Are You?

       Photo credit: Karla Doell

When No One Is Watching, people and their struggles go unnoticed. See them. Love them.

Stone Circle – Photo credit: Karla Doell

What If I Told You? What if you said "I love you" before they leave you to wonder if they ever knew?

       Photo credit: David Doell

Don't tell Kiera, but the *Watermelon Seeds* never grew.

A *Ball in the Yard* is bounce-bounce fun.

On the wooden *Door Frame* the height marks of three children are faithfully recorded to adulthood.

       Photo credit: Karla Doell

Children are the blank *Slate* you may use to observe the world.

       Art credit: Kiera Doell

Glade is a dilemma of strewn pedals and surrounding darkness.

Fire – Photo credit: Karla Doell
I originally wrote the first draft of *Not a Poem* thinking that it was not, in fact, a poem, hence the title. People may think poems have to adhere to a certain format; as I discovered, however, the requirements for poetry are as diverse as its poets.
I began with *The Blank Page*…and crafted this poem.

Logs – Photo credit: Karla Doell
The Perfect Season was originally written to answer the question, "What is your perfect season?"
The *Elaine Phillips* acrostic was inspired by my mentor and written in honour of her birthday.
      Photo credit: Karla Doell
Engineer's Birthday is written from the point of view of our family in attendance at my father's birthday. He is an engineer who has spent his time building treasures in heaven.
      Photo credit: Jeremy Doell
Hug was presented to my dad for Father's Day.

Embers/Coal/Ash – Photo credit: David Doell
For the Rest of Us was written, upon request, after my grandpa Doell's passing.
How Do I Say Goodbye? was inspired by a funeral sermon.
      Photo credit: Karla Doell
Your *Shadow* is only noticed in the light, but it is always there.
The Sound is my own convoluted construct.
If *Satan's Roller Coaster* is so destructive, why do we keep riding it?
      Photo credit: Jeremy Doell
There are consequences when you are *Too Weak to Stand* against injustice in society....
The *Temptation* kitty is watching you.
      Photo credit: Karla Doell
If Only I had that extra chance and one more breath…to complain about what I don't have.

Sparks – Photo credit: Jeremy Doell
Summer Skies is an imaginative and playful description of the clouds in summer.
In *Autumn* the leaves change colour and fall, ushering in a new season and anticipating winter's beauty.
       Photo credit: David Doell
Reprieve is specifically about the warm Chinook winds which blow in from the mountains. (The idea of what it takes to create a reprieve is something else entirely.)
Waves of Sand was written as an assignment to demonstrate my understanding of metaphor.
       Photo credit: Karla Doell
While driving in the car one winter, *Warm Snowfall* was sung—completely improvised—to my baby sister; later I wrote it down.
       Photo credit: David Doell
Lily Rose uses flower-imagery to visualize a person's spirit.
Shells of the Ocean is a word sonnet consisting of fourteen words with each one on a separate line.
       Photo credit: Karla Doell

(RE)KINDLING THE LIGHT

The leitmotif for this anthology began with a scene in my mind of a starry sky, above a stone circle, around a fire with logs and kindling used to start the flames. The overarching heavens seem a fitting location for the 'God poems' in the collection: tributes to the Creator and a secure belief in His perfect presence, beauty, sovereignty and eternal love. The stone circle offers both vulnerability and protection: here we find the 'children poems'. All is not sweetness and light; there is a dark side, too. As the fire loses its heat, embers turn to ash unless the flames are fanned. In the sparks, beyond the imagery, ideas take shape. Our eyes adjust to the dark and we see (again) the brightness that was always there.

Made in the USA
Charleston, SC
14 August 2014